BRITISH RAILWAYS

PAST and PRESENT

No 56

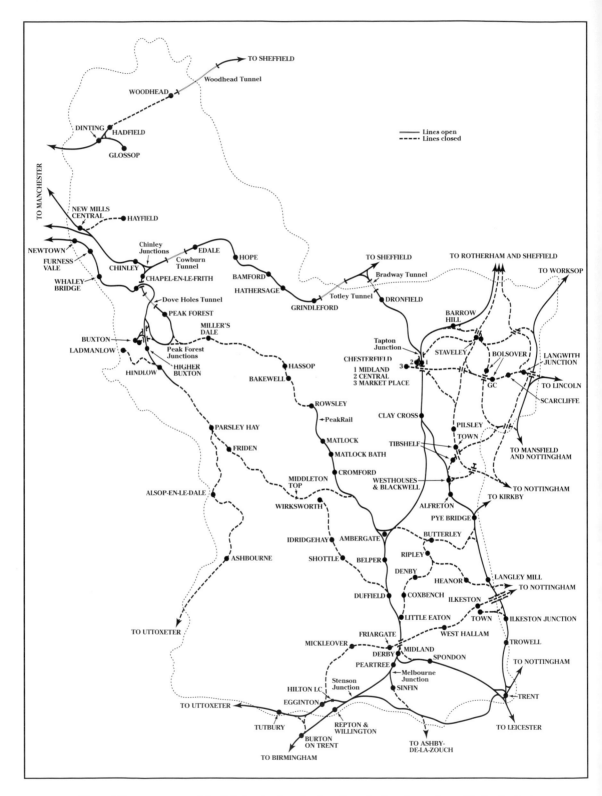

Map of the area covered by this book, showing locations featured or referred to in the text. For clarity some minor and colliery lines have been omitted.

BRITISH RAILWAYS

PAST and PRESENT

No 56

Derbyshire

John Hillmer

Past and
Present

Past & Present Publishing Ltd

This book is dedicated to my wife Geraldine for her constant support and tolerance

First published in 2007
Reprinted 2007

British Library Cataloguing in Publication Data

A catalogue record for this book is available from the British Library.

ISBN 978 1 85895 252 9

Past & Present Publishing Ltd
The Trundle
Ringstead Road
Great Addington
Kettering
Northants NN14 4BW

Tel/Fax: 01536 330588
email: sales@nostalgiacollection.com
Website: www.nostalgiacollection.com

Printed and bound in the Czech Republic

DERBY WORKS had a long history (dating back to 1840) of repairing and building steam locos for the North Midland Railway onwards through to diesels and units for British Railways, and the clock tower building of the Locomotive Works is perhaps the best-known part of the complex. Three locomotives were preserved at Derby, and in our 'past' picture we see MR 4-2-2 No 118 with the Works in the background (and a London, Tilbury & Southend Railway 4-4-2T to the right) on 15 February 1965.

The last operational shop (Bombardier) closed in October 2005, and there is now no railway activity within Pride Park. On 24 May 2006 Fragonset 'Peak' No 45112 *The Royal Army Ordnance Corps* stands in almost the identical position. *David Holmes/JCH*

CONTENTS

DERBY FRIARGATE was opened as plain 'Derby' by the Great Northern Railway in 1878, but was renamed Derby Friargate three years later. The prime purpose of the line was to gain access to Burton and elsewhere via Mickleover and Egginton Junction. The service was withdrawn by BR in 1964, although the station continued to be used for goods and excursion traffic until 1967. On 4 June 1950 'D2' 4-4-0 No 62172 (built at Doncaster in 1900 and the only member of the class to carry a BR number) is seen on the 10.10am (Sundays) train to Grantham.

Although the platforms remain in situ, access is not possible. In our first 'present' picture we see the premises using the arches below the former station and the chimneys of the station buildings. The second photo shows the beautifully preserved railway bridge over Friar Gate, looking away from the city centre. Both pictures were taken on 17 June 2005. *H. C. Casserley/JCH (2)*

INTRODUCTION

As most of the 'past' pictures in this book were taken in the second half of the 20th century, it is fitting to review that period in the long history of the railways of Derbyshire. During the Second World War railways in the UK worked to absolute capacity and undoubtedly were worn out at the end. One of the first Bills put through by the newly elected Labour Government led to nationalisation in 1945, which brought an end to the 'Big Four' formed in 1923, although the new British Railways Regions were based closely on the old company lines.

As people could once again travel freely, the railways enjoyed a boom period with coastal resorts being the favourite destinations. However, as more and more private cars began to appear, so began the decline in passenger numbers. Dr Beeching came long in the mid-1960s and his Report led to the closures of many lines. The first major loss in Derbyshire was that of the Midland main line through the Peak to Manchester, followed by that of the Woodhead line, of which only a small part was in the county, leaving the Hope Valley line as the only direct route from Manchester to Sheffield; the latter became an important hub for passengers wishing to travel south to Chesterfield, Derby and beyond. The position with freight was even worse, mainly because of the gradual closure of the pits to the point where there is now no coal produced in Derbyshire at all.

The huge former Midland Railway Works at Derby continued to build diesel locomotives and units after the cessation of steam, but gradually diminished year by year until there is now no railway activity, although two of the Works buildings remain and may well have listed status.

However, on the positive side the movement of limestone from the Buxton area and cement from Hope is very successful, to the extent that there are times when the Hope Valley line is getting close to capacity with the half-hourly express Trans-Pennine services, the stopping trains between Manchester and Sheffield and the stone and cement traffic. In addition it seems that passenger numbers are steadily increasing with more people using the trains. As our roads approach gridlock one can look into the future of the railways with a degree of optimism.

Mention must be made of the growing preservation scene in the county. PeakRail between Matlock and Rowsley, the Midland Railway Centre at Butterley, the relatively new Ecclesbourne Valley Railway based at Wirksworth, the Barrow Hill Roundhouse Centre and the well-established Crich Tramway Museum are all attracting increasing numbers of visitors. For anyone interested in the history of the Midland Railway, The Midland Railway Society is a must and can be contacted through their web site: www.midlandrailwaysociety.org.uk.

John Hillmer
Wilmslow

ACKNOWLEDGEMENTS

My thanks go to all those who have submitted 'past' photographs, without which there would no book! In the UK we are very fortunate to have had and to still have so many talented and determined photographers who have covered the constantly changing railway scene. Their efforts and skills enable us to see in pictures just how things have altered over the years. I am also indebted to those people who have given so freely of their time and knowledge to answer my constant queries during the compilation of this book: the members of the Derbyshire Railways Discussion Group (http:finance.groups.yahoo.com/group/derbyshirerailways) have always been there with rapid response; Barry Monkman, Ralph Rawlinson, Howard Sprenger and Bryan Wilson, whose conversance with Derbyshire and with its railways knows no bounds; and especially Glynn Waite, who has read the manuscript and made numerous suggestions, and whose encyclopaedic knowledge of the history of Derbyshire's railways (and of the Midland Railway in particular) is so incredibly full and detailed. However, it must be clearly stated that the responsibility for any errors in the captions is totally mine.

My thanks also go to Paul Shannon for his remarkable freight expertise and for help with the map, to Will Adams at Past & Present Publishing for his help and advice, and finally but not least to my wife Geraldine, for her digital scanning and printing skills and whose constant support is always there.

BIBLIOGRAPHY

ABC British Railways Locomotives, combined volumes, various years (Ian Allan)
Baker, S. K. *Rail Atlas Great Britain & Ireland*, various editions (OPC)
Bentley, J. M. *The Railway from Buxton to Bakewell, Matlock & Ambergate* (Foxline)
Butt, R. V. J. *Directory of Railway Stations* (Patrick Stephens Ltd)
Griffiths, Roger and Smith, Paul *Directory of British Engine Sheds, North Midlands, Northern England and Scotland* (OPC)
Jacobs, Gerald *Quail Track Diagrams/Midlands & North West* (Trackmaps)
Knighton, Laurence *Hassop – a Chronology of Railway History* (Midland Railway Society)
Leleux, Robin *A Regional History of the Railways of Great Britain Vol 9 East Midlands* (David St John Thomas)
Lund, Brian *Derbyshire Railway Stations on Old Picture Postcards* (Reflections of a Bygone Age)
Pritchard, Fox and Hall *BR Locos & Coaching Stock 2005* (Platform 5)
Rawlinson, Ralph *Railway Ramblers Gazetteer of Disused Lines* (www.railwayramblers.org.uk)
Shannon, Paul *Rail Freight Since 1968: Coal* (Silver Link Publishing)
Smith, Paul *Steam Motive Power Depots* (Platform 5)
Waite, Glynn *The Midland Railway on Old Picture Postcards* (Reflections of a Bygone Age)
Wignall, C. J. *Complete BR Maps and Gazetteer from 1830-1981* (OPC)

Lines around Derby

DERBY MIDLAND: The current station, which was built by the North Midland Railway, dates back to 1840, having replaced the Birmingham & Derby Junction station that had opened the previous year. The new station was built in a manner befitting the constituent of a company that was to become a major player in the railways of the UK – the Midland Railway. Taken on 16 April 1959, our 'past' picture shows the grand façade of the station, together with a Derby Corporation Daimler double-decker and the photographer's 1934 Hillman Minx (being driven by his son!).

The modern building is on much simpler lines but nonetheless has character. By the entrance are two beautiful coats of arms, which can be seen on either side of the Arriva double-decker. To the right is that of the city of Derby and to the left that of the Midland Railway, as seen in the inset. *H. C. Casserley/JCH (2)*

DERBY MIDLAND: On the lovely summer's day of 24 July 1955, looking north from the footbridge near the south end of the station, we see Class 5 4-6-0 No 44981 awaiting departure with an up semi-fast, while at the adjacent platform a Fowler 2-6-4T is shunting empty coaching stock, with another train further along. To the left are the extensive railway offices and on the far right lies Derby Locomotive Works.

Fifty years later, on 17 June 2005, it is only possible to get a similar view of the station from the bridge carrying London Road over the railway, but it is spoiled by the girder-type 'bridge' carrying pipes. Nonetheless we can see a great deal of activity: from left to right there is a track machine, a Midland Mainline HST, a Class 158 DMU in the distance, with a 170 unit to the right, then a Class 222, another HST and finally a Class 31 and Class 47 stabled on the extreme right. *Brian Morrison/JCH*

DERBY MIDLAND: At the north end, on 5 June 1965, Class 5 4-6-0 No 44945 approaches the station with the stock for the 08.40 train to Blackpool, having passed under several signal gantries with Derby Junction signal box on the right, and to the left part of the railway office buildings.

In the same view looking north on 26 August 2005, a Midland Mainline HST approaches with a Sheffield to St Pancras service. All the semaphores have been swept away and a new road crosses the railway, but the track layout appears to be little changed. *P. A. Forbes/JCH*

DERBY MIDLAND: Standing at Platform 4 in the spring of 1964 with a down parcels train is Ivatt 2-6-0 No 46402, carrying a 16C shed plate.

Due to station refurbishment, it was almost impossible to take a photo of a train at Platform 4, so from Platform 3, looking across, we see Midland Mainline Class 222 No 222010 awaiting departure for London St Pancras on 26 August 2005. These new units are known as 'Meridians', and are built by Bombardier in both four- and nine-car sets. *Keith Sanders/JCH*

DERBY MIDLAND: On 19 August 1958 Great Central Railway (GCR)-designed 'A5' 4-6-2T No 69820 arrives at Platform 2b with a service from Lincoln St Marks, which would have run via Newark Castle and Nottingham. Classes 'D11' and 'D16' were also used on these services.

On 24 May 2006, despite the continued refurbishment of Derby station, the view is unmistakeably the same, with Class 170/6 No 170635 arriving at Platform 2 with a Nottingham-Worcester service, operated by Central Trains. *Noel Machell/JCH*

DERBY SHED: The former North Midland Railway roundhouse was opposite the station, and on 29 June 1960 a line of ex-MR 0-6-0s stands in front of it, including No 43429 at the extreme left of the front row. The shed, whose LMS/BR shed code was 17A, closed in 1967 and was demolished two years later.

On 26 August 2005 there is no link with the past. The diesel stabling point is round to the left and on the right we can see a Midland Mainline HST approaching the station with a St Pancras-Sheffield service. *Ron Robinson/JCH*

APPROACHING DERBY: On 5 August 1978 'Peak' No 45039 *The Manchester Regiment*, with a down express consisting of ten coaches, probably from the South West, is photographed from Osmaston Road bridge near Derby station.

Today there is a very little difference. The large factory on the right, Ewart's of Derby (chain manufacturers), remains, although the furthest part has been demolished. Two-car Class 170 'Turbostar' unit No 170115, operated by Central Trains and based at Tyseley, is employed on a Crewe to Nottingham service on 27 October 2005. *Gavin Morrison/JCH*

APPROACHING DERBY: Class 25 No 25215 heads the SO 1300 Llandudno-Nottingham service on 5 August 1978. On the left-hand side is BR's Litchurch Lane Works, Apprentice Training School, while on the extreme right can be seen Charringtons oil terminal.

Just over 25 years later there has been very little change. The six tracks remain in place, although the two right-hand ones (St Andrews Nos 1 and 2 Sidings) see little or no use. It is likely that the area to the right will be used as the site for the planned new Derby Control Centre. A four-car Class 220 'Voyager' unit heads south with a Virgin CrossCountry service, seen from London Road bridge on 24 May 2006. *Gavin Morrison/JCH*

ILKESTON TOWN station was known as simply 'Ilkeston' when opened in 1847; the trains were initially horse-drawn, but the line closed in 1870. Re-opened as Ilkeston Town in 1879, connecting the town again with the nearby Ilkeston Junction station (in Nottinghamshire), some trains went through to Nottingham or Chesterfield. At 47 chains it was certainly the shortest station-to-station branch on the Midland Railway. It closed for passenger services in 1947, although it continued to be used for goods and excursion traffic until 1959. In our 'past' picture of 27 June 1933, Midland loco No 1403 is seen at the single platform with the 5.01pm train from Pye Bridge to Nottingham via Ilkeston. The wooden-bodied mineral wagon on the left bears the name 'Butterley'.

The station was situated near Bath Street, but today there is nothing to connect the past with the present as there has been a great deal of development in the area. However, a similar four-wheeled wagon, bearing the name 'Stanton Ironworks', has been mounted on one of the roundabouts (on Chalons Way, the A6007) close to the site of the station, which is a nice touch to remember the past, as seen on 20 October 2005. *H. C. Casserley/JCH*

SPONDON station is on the Derby-Nottingham main line via Trent Junction, and dates back to 1839, when it was opened by the Midland Counties Railway. It is rather a long walk from the village centre and probably owes its continued existence to the fact that it is close to the large former Courtaulds factory, which at one time produced acetate rayon yarn, was rail connected, and was also an oil terminal. In the photograph of 11 July 1986 Class 31 No 31326 approaches the sidings with 6T23, the 1343 Derby St Mary's-Toton Speedlink service, comprising barrier wagons and tanks containing chlorine and acetic acid.

Although the 'present' picture was taken less than 20 years later there have been considerable changes. The signal box and semaphore signals have all gone, and the nearby level crossing has CCTV and automatic barriers operated from Derby PSB and carries road traffic to the Acordis Tow-owned plant, which manufactures acetate for use in cigarette filters and exports its products all over the world. The sidings remain in situ, but on 20 October 2005 the rails looked very rusty and, apart from a trial delivery of oil from Immingham during that year, there has been no traffic since 2002. A four-car Midland Mainline Class 222 'Meridian' unit approaches with an up service. *Paul Shannon/JCH*

SPONDON station is seen on 27 June 1983 looking towards Trent. A three-car Class 120 with M56354 leading is about to stop en route to Derby (where it will reverse), forming the 1620 Nottingham to Birmingham New Street service. The large factory buildings can be seen on the right, with a number of tank wagons in the sidings. The station has an attractive waiting room on the Derby-bound platform.

Today there is an intermittent service of stopping trains, amounting on weekdays to seven in each direction, operated by Central Trains, but there are some considerable gaps; for instance, In the Nottingham-Derby direction there is a break of 6 hours after the 1132 service. There was a bay at one time on the westbound side, which was used by workmen's trains for employees at the British Celanese factory. The station has had a 'make-over' as we can see from the 'present' photograph of 20 October 2005, with Class 156 No 156143 heading towards Derby. *Brian Morrison/JCH*

PEARTREE station lies to the south of Derby on the route to Burton-on-Trent. Opened as Pear Tree & Normanton by the Midland Railway in 1890, it closed in 1968. Re-opened as just Peartree in 1976 for the Sinfin services – although that branch is closed to passenger traffic – it remains open. In the 'past' photo we see Kirtley '700' Class standard goods 0-6-0 No 2858 passing through the station towards Derby with a platelayers train in about 1920. The wooden hut by the bridge is likely to have been the booking office.

On 27 October 2005 a Virgin 'Voyager' speeds through with a CrossCountry service. The station has been modernised, but the Osmaston Park Road bridge remains. Today's service is just two stopping trains in each direction Monday to Saturday. *H. L. Salmon, courtesy of R. M. Casserley/JCH*

MELBOURNE JUNCTION is where the Chellaston line (later to be the Sinfin branch) left the main line from Derby to Burton-on-Trent. In our first 'past' picture, taken on 6 March 1966, 'Peak' No D111 is at the head of the diverted 1400 Manchester Central to St Pancras train as it passes the Midland-style signal box on to the branch. A North Western Road Car Company Leyland Tiger Cub is parked nearby.

The second photo was taken 17 years later, on 1 July 1983, and shows Class 56 No 56010 with a loaded MGR train as it travels south.

On 27 October 2005 the scene is very pastoral and only a distant chimney remains as a Virgin 'Voyager' passes the junction on its way south towards Burton. The branch line was cut back to Sinfin Central, the passenger service ending in 1993, and there is now only an occasional oil train to Rolls Royce. *P. A. Forbes/Brian Morrison/ JCH*

SINFIN CENTRAL and Sinfin North were the only two stations on the branch, primarily used for workers at Rolls Royce. On 1 July 1983 a three-car Class 120 (M56392 leading) is seen at Central station before returning to Derby. The stations closed in 1993, but Rolls Royce still receives deliveries of oil, currently sourced from Grangemouth.

The remains of the station lie within the works complex, which is not accessible, but our 'present' photo of 27 October 2005 is taken from where the single line crossed Wilmore Road. Looking towards the station, this is literally the end of the line as, on the other side of the road, the track ends and is now a path. *Brian Morrison/JCH*

South-west of Derby

TUTBURY station is just in Derbyshire, a matter of 100 yards from the River Dove, which forms the boundary with Staffordshire. The line from Stoke to Derby was opened in 1848 by the North Staffordshire Railway; passenger services were withdrawn by BR in 1966, before a completely new station was opened as 'Tutbury & Hatton' in 1989. The platforms are no longer opposite one another and entry is gained to both from the road crossing, controlled by Tutbury Crossing signal box. In the photograph taken in the early 1900s, looking towards Derby, the chimney of Nestlé's factory (built in 1901) can be seen beyond the station. There is a back platform on the up side that was used for trains to Burton-on-Trent; the platforms have awnings, a footbridge by the crossing and no doubt a large station staff.

The second 'past' photo is the view from a footbridge, looking in the same direction with two signal boxes on the up side, and the yard on the right where J. C. Staton & Co's (plaster works) line entered from across the river; the supports for its bridge can still be seen to this day. At this time the station was none-existent.

In the 'present' picture, taken on 15 February 2006, the photographer is standing near the east end of the down platform (to Stoke) as Class 170 'Turbostar' No 170115 stops with the 0907 service from Crewe to Derby, operated by Central Trains. The crossing box (dating back to c1872) and the Nestlé's factory remain much the same, but there are now no sidings whatsoever. Nestlé began processing milk from local farms in 1901, using the NSR for distribution. Extensively rebuilt in the 1950s, from 1959 the factory began the manufacture of instant coffee. *Lens of Sutton/Roger Newman collection/JCH*

TUTBURY: Looking towards Uttoxeter on 27 June 1933, LNER 'J3' 0-6-0 No 4094 (dating from 1897) enters the station with the 9.03am train from Stafford to Derby (Friargate) – these trains were operated by the GNR. There is a milk tank behind the loco, which must have been fairly new as until the 1920s all milk traffic was conveyed in churns. The carriages are an articulated pair, rebuilt from a couple of GNR six-wheelers of the 1880s/'90s. To the left of the train is the entrance to the marshalling sidings, where the line from J. C. Staton's came in from across the river. The station nameboard says 'Tutbury change For Burton'.

More than 70 years later, on 15 February 2006, the line remains dead straight but there is nothing left to link the view with the 'past' picture. 'Turbostar' No 170115 is arriving as the 0907 service from Crewe to Derby – the platforms of the new station are no longer opposite one another. *H. C. Casserley/JCH*

TUTBURY: This wonderful photograph of Class 8F 2-8-0 No 48332 on a long mixed goods forging westwards through the station on a frosty 27 December 1965 (again looking towards Derby) is too good to leave out. *P. A. Forbes*

EGGINTON JUNCTION was where the Derby Friargate line left that from Stoke to Derby. Opened by the Great Northern Railway in 1878, and operated jointly with the North Staffordshire Railway, it remained open until 1962. Regular passenger trains on the GNR side had ceased in 1939, although the seasonal Kings Norton-Skegness service called until September 1961. In the 'past' picture of 9 August 1966, Class 25 No D5268 is on the GNR line marshalling a train carrying BMC cars. In the distance on the right can be seen Egginton Junction signal box, while on the left is the original station building.

On 16 February 2006 the alignment of the railway could still be seen, and the station building has been beautifully restored, lying within its own grounds. The signal box remains, although obscured by the trees. *P. A. Forbes/JCH*

HILTON LEVEL CROSSING: The 'past' photograph was taken in 1975 from the north side of the line, showing the small crossing box that controlled the gates. The sign on the right once read 'Egginton Junction Station', which was situated a couple of hundred yards to the right.

Thirty-one years later, on 16 February 2006, the scene looks much the same, but the small box has been replaced by a modern 'Portakabin' to the left of the gates, which are still operated manually by the crossing-keeper. *Michael Mensing/JCH*

REPTON & WILLINGTON station is on the main line from Burton-on-Trent to Derby, south-west of Stenson Junction. The original station was opened in 1839 by the Birmingham & Derby Junction Railway as plain 'Willington', renamed in 1877 to 'Repton & Willington', then 'Willington for Repton' in 1889, the Midland Railway eventually reverting to 'Repton & Willington'. On 15 April 1957 a goods train is approaching hauled by ex-Midland 0-6-0 No 43826.

The station closed in 1968, but up on the embankment a modern new station was opened in 1995, now called simply 'Willington' with minimum facilities. On 5 February 2006 Central Trains Class 170 No 170113 approaches from the Burton-on-Trent direction, but few trains on the Cardiff to Nottingham route stop here. *Milepost 92½ (H. B. Priestley collection)/JCH*

WILLINGTON POWER STATION was situated on the south side of the Burton to Derby line, a few hundred yards to the west of Stenson Junction. In the photo of 2 August 1984 Nos 25302+25285 approach with 8E36, the 1810 Longport to Worksop service, carrying sand from Cauldon Low to Worksop for glassmaking. To the left can be seen the lines into the power station.

The power station closed in 1999, two of the cooling towers were demolished in 2001, and the lines into the power station have been lifted. Other than that the view remains much the same on 16 February 2006 as Class 66/6 No 66605 in Freightliner livery heads 6E54, the 1038 Kingsbury to Humber Oil Refinery empty bogie tanks. *Paul Shannon/JCH*

Midland main line: Derby to Ambergate and the Denby and Wirksworth branches

LITTLE EATON: On 11 July 1986 Nos 20149+20140 are at the head of 6L54 from Denby opencast disposal point to Lea Hall Colliery, from where the coal will be moved by conveyer belt to Rugeley Power Station. The signal box looks rather the worse for wear, having closed in 1969!

Getting on for 20 years later, on 16 August 2005, the line is disused, although the track remains. The signal box has been demolished. *Paul Shannon/JCH*

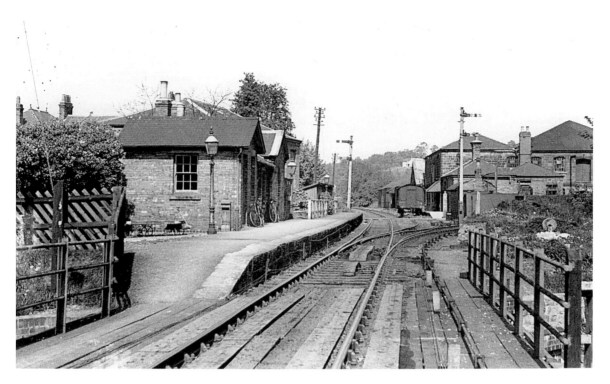

LITTLE EATON station was the first on the Ripley branch, which left the Midland main line between Derby and Duffield at Little Eaton Junction. Opened in 1856, it lasted for passenger services until 1930. This photograph, taken in May 1946 looking towards Denby, depicts the delightful scene of a single-platform country station, with sidings entering the Brook Mill paper mill.

Nearly 60 years later, on 23 April 2006, the scene is unrecognisable, but the building on the right was the Station House, although it was on the opposite side of the track from the station platform. *H. C. Casserley/JCH*

COXBENCH station was the next to the north, again opened in 1856 and remaining open until 1930. On 8 July 1993 Class 58 No 58004 is taking empties to Denby, which will be loaded with coal, then worked to Drakelow Power Station. The house is occupied and the platform used for attractive floral displays.

The last coal train from Denby ran in April 1999, but the station building remains in private hands, as seen in the 'present' picture of 17 August 2005. The major difference is that the left-hand wooden gate has been replaced by a metal one! *Paul Shannon/JCH*

DUFFIELD is north of Derby on the main line to Chesterfield. The first station was opened by the North Midland Railway in 1841, and closed in 1867 when a new one was built to the south, in connection with the opening of the Wirksworth branch' the actual junction for the branch (taken out in 2003) was just south of the station. On 27 June 1983 'Peak' No 45038 is rather 'overkill' for a three-coach southbound parcels train. On the right, just beyond the trees, lies St Alkmund's, Duffield's parish church.

In the 'present' picture, taken on 16 August 2005, a Virgin 'Voyager' passes with the 0844 York to Derby service. The principal difference is that the goods/slow line on the down side has been removed. This gave access to the Wirksworth branch and also allowed the occasional passenger movement into the station to enable a fast train to pass. *Brian Morrison/JCH*

SHOTTLE was the second station on the Wirksworth branch, opened in 1867 and closed to passengers in 1947 (last train), but officially not until 1949. However, it remained open for freight, and on 29 October 1986 'Peak' No 45146 passes the station buildings with 8P07, a loaded limestone train from the quarry at Wirksworth. Formed of 21 HKV ex-ironstone hoppers bound for Derby St Mary's yard, it is destined ultimately for the British Sugar works at South Lynn.

This traffic last ran in 1990, after which the branch fell into disuse, but the track remains in situ, as seen in the 'present' photograph of 16 August 2005. As would be expected, there has been a considerable growth of trees and bushes in the intervening 19 years. Happily, the future looks bright as part of the Ecclesbourne Valley Railway. *Paul Shannon/JCH*

IDRIDGEHAY lay between Shottle and Wirksworth, the station opening in 1867 and officially closing to passenger traffic in 1949. It is said that the station used to be an important meeting place for farmers, who brought their milk for transportation to London and Sheffield. The 'past' photograph is of LMS 2-6-2T No 1205 heading for Wirksworth.

The last freight train ran in 1990, but on 16 August 2005 everything looks smart and tidy. The station house is in private hands and has had a small extension added, while the crossing is now AOCL (Automatic Open Crossing monitored Locally by the train crew). The solar-powered panels for the ungated level crossing can be seen opposite the platform; this unusual feature was introduced by British Rail. *J. C. Flemons courtesy of The Transport Treasury/JCH*

WIRKSWORTH was the terminus of the branch, and opened with it in 1867; the last passenger train ran in 1947, although official closure was not until 1949. The quarry remained open and on 15 April 1983 we see Class 31 No 31293 with four MSV covered wagons. Originally tipplers, they have been redeployed in general stone traffic, for discharge by mechanical grab.

The line closed to all traffic in 1991, and by 16 August 2005 there has been remarkable change. Although the quarry rail traffic has ended, parts of the infrastructure remain. Wyvern Rail and its volunteer support group, the Ecclesbourne Valley Railway Association, was formed to revive the line, and as can be seen a station has been built together with track modifications. Single-car GRCW Class 122 No 55006 is in the station and is running a shuttle service to Gorsey Bank and back (with the blind showing the unlikely destination of Penzance!). Preserved Class 31 No 31414 can also be seen, and on the far right the line continues on with a shunter visible. By September 2005 trains were running from Wirksworth to Ravenstor, the final object being to restore services on the 8-mile branch. Since the photograph was taken the Dust Dock building has been removed. *Paul Shannon/JCH*

BELPER lies between Duffield and Ambergate on the main line. The first station was opened by the North Midland Railway in 1840, then closed in 1878 when it was replaced by a new one in King Street. On 4 May 1934 LMS 'Crab' 2-6-0 No 13147 (built in 1930) heads south with a mixed goods train.

More than 50 years later, while the station has been refurbished and there has been considerable tree growth, the scene is much the same, although the length of the platforms was reduced in the 1970s. A Virgin Class 221 'Voyager' is about to pass through the station with a Cross Country service. Apart from a Midland Mainline train, which stops en route to St Pancras, and a Sheffield service in the morning, the town is served by Derby-Matlock trains, which are two-hourly. *H. C. Casserley/JCH*

Midland main line: north to Chesterfield and Dronfield

CHESTERFIELD: In 1840 the North Midland Railway opened the first station, replaced in 1870 by a second, 90 metres to the north; this was renamed Chesterfield St Mary's in 1950, but only until 1951, then to Chesterfield Midland before becoming simply Chesterfield (again) in 1964, following the closure of Central station. On 9 April 1977 Class 45/1 'Peak' No 45144 *Royal Signals* from Toton is about to leave with a Glasgow-Nottingham service.

Twenty-eight years later, on 17 June 2005, Class 60 No 60013 *Robert Boyle* is seen bringing a long train of bogie wagons through the station. To the right of the up platform are the freight-only lines from Barrow Hill and Rotherham. The station is very well kept – note the beautifully decorated pillars. *Both JCH*

CHESTERFIELD: On 4 June 1977 double-headed Class 25s (Nos 25159+25124) head north with a rake of six Mark I coaches. Looking back on the notes from that day, there was a wonderful variety of diesels – Classes 31, 37, 40, 45, 46 and 47, with 'Peaks' predominating. The large works in the background was Markham's, a general heavy engineering company, whose most famous contract was probably one of its last – the UK tunnel boring machines for Eurotunnel.

On 17 June 2005 we see Class 170/5 'Turbostar' No 170519, operated by Central Trains, departing as a Liverpool-Norwich service. There has been some track rationalisation and the works behind the train has been demolished following closure in 1999. *Both JCH*

CHESTERFIELD: The exterior of the Midland station is seen on 9 June 1956. When it was being planned, it was described as being 'Gothic in style, consisting of three parts, the central one being the booking hall two storeys high, the south wing will contain the waiting rooms and the north wing the stations master's, parcels, telegraph and porters rooms.'

In 1963-65 the station was demolished and rebuilt, then in 1992 alterations costing £300,000 were put in motion. The results are seen in the view taken on 13 September 2005, showing the attractive modern frontage. The inset shows the statue of George Stephenson outside the station – he was not a native of the town, but during his illustrious railway career, including being Chief Engineer of the North Midland Railway, he bought Tapton House in 1838; he died there in 1848 and is buried in Chesterfield. *H. C. Casserley/JCH*

CHESTERFIELD MARKET PLACE station was opened by the Lancashire, Derbyshire & East Coast Railway in 1897, and was the terminus of a line that ran from Lincoln. It was not known as 'Market Place' until ten years later, when the company was absorbed by the Great Central Railway. The GCR now had to add suffixes, as it had two Chesterfield stations: the Manchester, Sheffield & Lincolnshire Railway (MS&LR)/GCR station thus became 'Central'. Market Place remained open for passenger traffic until 1951 and for goods until 1957. As seen in the 'past' picture of 7 June 1956, the station had a very imposing façade with the Portland Hotel next door.

On 13 September 2005 the scene shows nothing of the station, although the hotel can be seen beyond the trees. *H. C. Casserley/JCH*

CHESTERFIELD MARKET PLACE: Former GCR 4-6-2T (later 'A5') No 69821 waits with the 4.10pm service to Langwith Junction on 3 April 1951, the last year of operation. In the far distance can be seen the Town Hall, and to the right is the Portland Hotel.

There has been a considerable amount of redevelopment, and in the photograph of 10 October 2005 the site of the station is now partly a car park, but is clearly located once again by the Portland Hotel to the right and the Town Hall in the distance. *Milepost 92½ (H. B. Priestley)/JCH*

Below The dismantling of Market Place station, with the signal box looking the worse for wear. *H. C. Casserley*

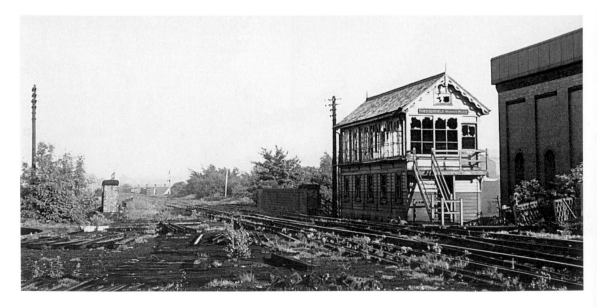

CHESTERFIELD CENTRAL station was opened by the Manchester, Sheffield & Lincolnshire Railway in 1893, the line forming a loop off the company's Sheffield to Nottingham main line in order to serve the town. The line closed to passenger traffic in 1963, although goods continued until 1964 (to the south) and 1967 (to the north). In this view ex-LNER 'B1' 4-6-0 No 61313 enters the station with the 10.05am (Sundays) Sheffield Victoria to Nottingham Victoria service on 3 November 1957. There is a bay platform to the left and what appears to be a goods yard to the right of the signal box.

Today nothing remains, the line of the track having been used for the A61 bypass, as seen in the photograph of 8 July 2005, looking north, although between Mill Street and St Mary's Gate there still remains a reminder of the past in 'Station Road'. *David Holmes/JCH*

CHESTERFIELD: A few hundred yards north of the Midland station there is a well-known footbridge that has been popular with photographers for many years. On 17 May 1966 ex-LMS 8F 2-8-0 No 48067 passes with a down mixed goods train. The station can be seen in the distance, with a clutch of semaphore signals. Two sets of sidings are visible.

On the afternoon of 10 October 2005, nearly 40 years on, Class 66 No 66028 is at the head of the Toton-Castleton (Lancs) engineer's train of bogies carrying rails, while in the station a Midland Mainline HST forms a Sheffield-St Pancras service. There is now a crossover in the foreground but the sidings have gone. *Roger Siviter/JCH*

DRONFIELD lies between Sheffield and Chesterfield, and on 3 October 1959, just to the north of the station, BR Standard 5MT 4-6-0 No 73156 is seen with an up fitted goods.

The tree growth has been considerable during the 46 years to 8 July 2005, as a Midland Mainline HST forms the 1227 Sheffield to St Pancras service. This TOC continues to operate a fleet of HSTs although the Class 222 'Meridians' are now working a number of these services to the capital. *Michael Mensing/JCH*

East of Chesterfield

SCARCLIFFE station was on the line from Chesterfield Market Place to Langwith Junction and beyond. Opened in 1898 by the Lancashire, Derbyshire & East Coast Railway, it survived ownership by the Great Central and the LNER before being finally closed by BR in 1951. In the 'past' photo, taken on 18 May 1951, one of the crew of the Great Central-designed 4-6-2T that became BR 'A5' No 69812 is about to give up the tablet with the 9.40am Chesterfield Market Place to Langwith Junction service.

There is nothing to relate to in the 'present' picture of 10 October 2005, but the third view shows that the station house is well preserved and in use as a private residence. *Milepost 92½ (H. B. Priestley)/JCH (2)*

BOLSOVER GC was the next station to the west, opened in 1897 and having a name change to Bolsover South in 1950, but closing in December of the following year. Looking towards Chesterfield, the 'past' picture was taken on 30 March 1951 and shows ex-LNER Class '04/7' 2-8-0 No 63588 with an eastbound mineral train.

Today, with the exception of the Station House, photographed on 18 May 2006, there is nothing left to be seen of the railway presence. *Milepost 92½ (H. B. Priestley)/JCH*

BOLSOVER COLLIERY AND COALITE PLANT were situated at the end of a short branch line from Seymour Junction, not far from Barrow Hill. On 18 December 1992 Class 58 No 58017 has just left the colliery with a train of coal for Ratcliffe Power Station. On the right is Bolsover Coalite smokeless fuel plant, which used a large number of items of ex-BR vintage rolling-stock for internal movements. In the background Bolsover Castle stands out on the skyline.

Today, although the track remains in situ, the Colliery and the Coalite plant have closed, as seen on 17 May 2006, being far outstripped in longevity by the remains of the 17th-century castle. It is remarkable how quickly nature can take over. *Paul Shannon/JCH*

BARROW HILL SHED was opened by the Midland Railway in 1870, consisting of a square brick building containing a turntable. Closed to steam in 1965, it continued as a diesel depot, becoming the only operational shed of its type. Downgraded to a stabling point in 1987, it finally closed in 1991. In the interior of the 'roundhouse', on 3 December 1961, is Johnson-designed 0-6-0 No 41804. This particular example was rebuilt with a Belpaire boiler, the Class having been originally introduced in 1878.

By a remarkable coincidence, in the 'present' photo, taken on 23 April 2006, another example of the Class was on view – No 41708. Both engines carry LMS worksplates 'Built at Derby', although both were built by the Midland Railway. The shed is now operated very successfully by Barrow Hill Engine Shed Society, who restored it to its former state, re-opening in 1998. It is usually open to the public at weekends. *Noel Machell/JCH, courtesy of the Barrow Hill Roundhouse Centre*

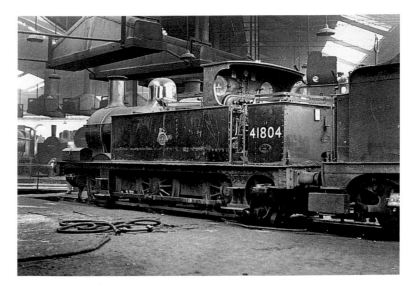

Below On 25 October 1959, outside the shed, are three 0-6-0 'Jinties' – Nos 47626, 47545 and 47620 – all carrying the 'lion and wheel' emblem. These engines were the mainstay shunting engines of the LMS; there were nearly 500 of them, having been originally designed by Johnson for the Midland Railway. *Noel Machell*

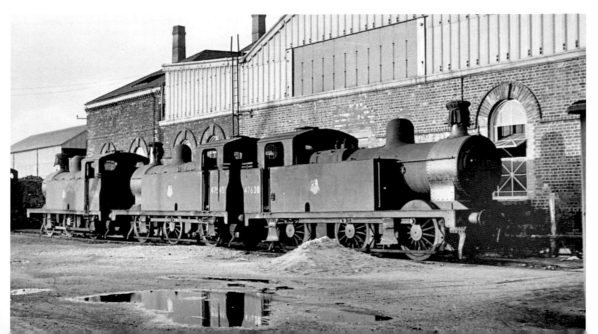

BARROW HILL station was on the line from Tapton Junction, just north of Chesterfield, to Rotherham (called the 'old road'). It was the second station, having been re-sited in 1888. Originally named 'Staveley', it then became 'Barrow Hill & Staveley Works' in 1900, until shortened to 'Barrow Hill' in 1951, closure coming in 1954. Twenty-five years ago, on 27 July 1981, looking in a south-westerly direction, there were two signal boxes and a myriad of semaphore signals as a Class 47 passes with six coaches. Off to the left is the freight-only line to Bolsover.

By the date of the second picture, 30 June 1983, there had already been considerable simplification of trackwork, the signal boxes had gone, and the semaphores replaced by colour lights. Class 47/3 No 47375 takes the freight-only branch with an empty MGR train.

On 22 April 2006 the platform has been removed but otherwise there is little change. The line to Bolsover remains, but appears to be unused, as a Class 60 passes the junction at the head of a train of TEA and TDA tank bogie wagons.
Paul Shannon/Brian Morrison/JCH

BARROW HILL: Looking in the opposite direction, 'Peak' No 45057 is seen with an up ballast empties working on 27 July 1981.

On 22 April 2006 the semaphores have been replaced by colour lights and the signal box is gone, but what appears at first glance to be a church on top of the hill remains. In fact, it is a primary school, but when built in 1856 the locals said that it looked liked a school, and as a school it looked like a church! It seems that a new church was built in 1895, so the original building became a totally dedicated primary school. The 'past' picture was taken from the footbridge which has subsequently been demolished, so the equivalent photo was taken from the bridge in the background of the earlier picture. The end of a train of tankers is disappearing, headed by a Class 60. *Paul Shannon/JCH*

TIBSHELF TOWN station was between Nottingham Victoria and Chesterfield Central, opened in 1893 by the MS&LR and closed in 1963. The route was part of the GCR main line between Manchester/Sheffield and Marylebone, and at Tibshelf was in a cutting that went under the town's High Street (B6014). In the 'past' photo 'B1' 4-6-0 No 61111 approaches Tibshelf Town station on 29 September 1959 with the 2.17pm Sheffield Victoria to Nottingham Victoria train. Apart from the varied passenger services most of the freight consisted of coal trains.

The last track was lifted in 1988, and today it is hardly credible but the whole of the cutting has been filled in and landscaped, becoming part of the 5 Pits Trail. As can be imagined it was virtually impossible to re-photograph the scene, but the church remains as do the buildings to the right, while the bridge behind the telegraph pole is the main road – this bridge still exists, as seen in the photo taken on 22 April 2006. *Michael Mensing/JCH*

PILSLEY station was the next station north on the GC main line; also opened by the MS&LR in 1893, it remained open until 1959. The 'past' picture shows the substantial platform buildings, with the booking office at road level above the lines.

   Today nothing remains of the railway, although the 5 Pits Trail follows the alignment. However, linking the two pictures on 17 May 2006 is the building to the left of the station, which survives and is more than 100 years old.
Lens of Sutton/JCH

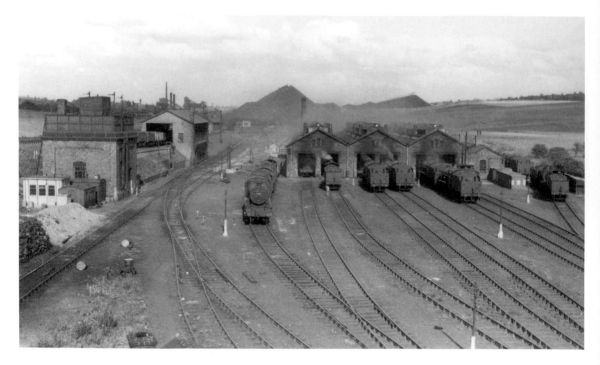

WESTHOUSES SHED was near Westhouses & Blackwell station. A brick-built 6TS dead-ended shed, it opened in 1890 and closed to steam in 1966, but continued as a diesel depot until about 1985, then was subsequently demolished. Primarily a freight shed, in the first photo we see a variety of steam locos on 8 July 1951. On the left is the ramped coaler and water tank, and there was also a 50-foot turntable.

In the second view, dated 29 June 1983, it can be seen that most of the shed has gone, with just two Class 20s (Nos 20193 and 20163) stabled.

On 17 May 2006, apart from the remains of the concrete walkways, there was nothing to be seen – nature had fully taken over. *John Ward collection/Brian Morrison/JCH*

ALFRETON station lies between Chesterfield and Nottingham. Dating back to 1862, it was re-named 'Alfreton & South Normanton' in 1891. Closed in 1967, it re-opened in 1973 as a 'Park & Ride' station, known as 'Alfreton & Mansfield Parkway'. On 24 July 1984 Class 47 No 47433 is at the head of the 1009 Barrow-in-Furness to Nottingham train.

Mansfield regained its own railway station when the line from Nottingham to Worksop was opened (the 'Robin Hood Line'), so the station name reverted to the simple 'Alfreton', with an hourly Norwich/Nottingham to Liverpool service operated by Central Trains. On 13 September 2005 a Class 170 unit is about to continue northwards. *Paul Shannon/JCH*

BENNERLEY is between Langley Mill and Trowell Junction on the direct Chesterfield to Nottingham route (the Erewash Valley line). On 28 June 1983 Nos 37122 (leading) and 37169 head south with a coal train. Behind is the remarkable viaduct that carried the GNR's Derby Friargate to New Basford line, and through the spans can be seen the Bennerley coal loading and blending complex (since closed), which was adjacent to the MR's line to Basford, which closed to passenger traffic on 1 January 1917. The viaduct is nearly 1,500 feet in length, made of iron because the ground would not take brick supports. It crosses two canals, the River Erewash and the Midland main line.

Although the GNR line closed to passenger traffic in 1964 (and completely in 1968), the viaduct remains, as seen in the 'present' picture taken 42 years later on 22 April 2006. In 1998 the ownership of this Grade II-listed structure passed to Sustrans. On 23 April 2006 a two-car Class 158 unit heads south. *Brian Morrison/JCH*

Left This close-up of the footbridge that can be seen beyond the viaduct was taken on 28 June 1983, with a Derby Class 114 twin unit (DTC No 50419 leading) forming a Sheffield-Nottingham service. *Brian Morrison*

RIPLEY: The first station was opened by the Midland Railway in 1856, but closed in 1889 to be replaced by a second the same year as the Heanor line opened. It remained open until 1930 for regular traffic, and at least 1961 for excursions. On 7 June 1926 No 1365 is working the 8.50am train from Derby.

Today little is to be seen of the station – just a couple of stone walls – but the road bridge over the railway remains in use, as seen in the picture taken on 7 June 2006, exactly 80 years to the day later! Nearby there is a Midland Hotel, no doubt named for the station. *H. C. Casserley/JCH*

WEST HALLAM (for Dale Abbey) was a GNR station between Nottingham Victoria and Derby Friargate; it opened in 1878 and survived until 1964. Two years before closure, on 7 May 1962, ex-LNER 'L1' 2-6-4T No 67745, of which 100 were built and which was no doubt allocated to Colwick shed, has arrived with the 4.12pm Derby Friargate-Grantham train.

Today all that remains is Station House, as seen on 23 April 2006, now in use as a Garden Centre, as shown in the third view. *H .F. Wheeller collection per R. S. Carpenter/JCH (2)*

Midland Railway through the Peak

AMBERGATE: Approaching from the south the line divided, with the Midland Railway main line to Matlock and Manchester Central going off to the left and the Sheffield line to the right, with a connecting line that ran east to Butterley and beyond. This triangular station opened in 1876, but only the former up Manchester platform now remains. In 1966 a Class 25 heads south with a mixed train of passenger coaches and parcel vans from the Manchester direction. To the left of the train, in the fork of the lines, can be seen the remains of the second (1863) station.

There has been huge tree growth in the 39 years to 26 August 2005 and as a consequence, although houses can be seen on the far side of the river valley, the railway is completely hidden. *Michael Mensing/JCH*

AMBERGATE was an important station, with a triangle of platforms and additional avoiding lines. No fewer than three stations were built, starting in 1840 (then 'Amber Gate'). The whole of the station triangle can be seen in this picture, looking north-west with the Matlock line disappearing away from the photographer, just to the right of centre. *John Ryan Collection*

AMBERGATE: Looking south, LMS-built three-cylinder 4P Compound 4-4-0 No 1063 approaches with a Derby-Manchester Central service in 1932. These engines were a post-Grouping development of the Johnson Midland Compound, and as late as 1956 there were nearly 200 of them running.

Today only one platform is needed, as the whole branch has been singled. On 22 April 2006 Class 158 No 158857 has just arrived with the 0702 service from Derby en route to Matlock. Although there is nothing on the station to link the pictures, to the right of the unit can be seen a building that is just visible to the right of the Compound in the 'past' photograph. *E. R. Morten/JCH*

AMBERGATE: Looking in the other direction towards Matlock, ex-Midland 4F 0-6-0 No 4407 enters the station with an up express in 1937. This was a Heaton Mersey engine and the service is possibly the 12.30pm SO Blackpool North to Desford dated train. In the LMS timetable of 1947 there were ten trains stopping in each direction, Monday to Saturday.

The footbridge having been removed, the nearest 'present' equivalent view is from the platform level of the current station, with Class 158 No 158794 (allocated to Tyseley) leaving for Matlock with a service from Derby on 26 August 2005. *E. R. Morten/JCH*

CROMFORD station opened in 1849 and has remained so ever since, making it well over 150 years of age! The up-side buildings date back to 1860, the down-side buildings from 1874, and the footbridge from 1885. In the 'past' picture, dating from 21 March 1986, one of the prototype Class 151 'Sprinters', No 151002, is seen with a Matlock-bound service. It was not followed by a production order and lasted only a few years in service.

On 21 September Class 170 'Turbostar' No 170512 is about to leave for Matlock, where the branch now terminates. There has been little change in the intervening 20 years, the only difference being that the bridge over the line is now private, being the entrance to the former Station Master's house, so the old up platform is inaccessible. *Paul Shannon/JCH*

HIGH TOR NO 1 TUNNEL is situated between Matlock Bath and Matlock. In the 'past' picture, taken from the end of Matlock Bath platform looking north, ex-MR 4F 0-6-0 No 3982 emerges. The date is unknown, but post-nationalisation as former LMS engines were given a '4' prefix; we therefore have to assume that the photograph was taken by the late 1940s. By the signal on the left is a fogman's hut.

Matlock Bath station dates back to 1849, and was closed by BR in 1967; however, it re-opened in 1972 and remains in service today, although only a single platform and un-staffed. The length of the old down platform is surprising, although today it is normally only used by two-car or three-car DMUs. On 24 May 2006 a Class 170 unit approaches forming the 1312 Matlock-Derby service. *R. S. Carpenter (D. Ibbotson collection)/JCH*

MATLOCK station was originally opened as 'Matlock Bridge' in 1849 by the Manchester, Buxton, Matlock & Midlands Junction Railway, and was re-named to the present title in 1905. After the closure of the former Midland Railway main line through the Peak, the station remained open (to Derby), but was closed to goods in 1972. On 4 September 1980, looking towards Cromford, a three-car DMU awaits departure forming the 1500 service to Derby. The line has been singled and only one platform remains in use. On the hillside beyond can be seen Riber Castle.

Almost exactly 25 years later there has been little change. The remains of the old down platform are inaccessible, so the angle of the photograph is a little different. Class 170 No 170514 forms the 1314 service to Derby. The Summer 2006 timetable consisted of 11 trains in each direction, Monday to Saturday. On Sundays this was reduced to seven, nearly all of which were from or to Nottingham, and operated by Central Trains. *Brian Morrison/JCH*

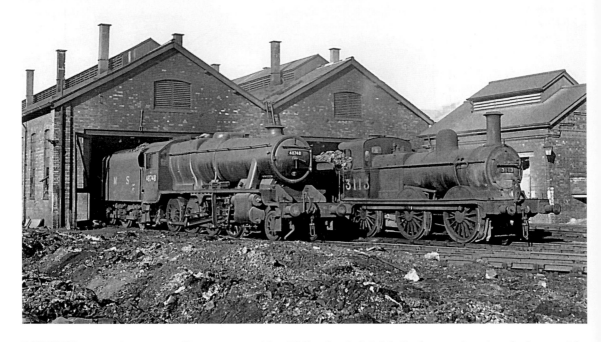

ROWSLEY was an important railway centre, with a Midland-style brick-built, four-road engine shed opened by the LMS in 1926. The facilities included a coal stage, water tank and turntable. Closed by BR in 1964, it remained as a signing-on point, with outbased Derby engines (both steam and diesel, the latter for passenger trains) stabled here until 1965. Diesels eventually took over the banking duties from steam, and were stabled near the coaling plant. Final closure came on 3 October 1966, and the building was subsequently demolished. In the photograph of 27 February 1949, on the left is ex-LMS 8F 2-8-0 No 48748, and on the right 2F 0-6-0 No 3113 (which became BR No 58244).

Rowsley is currently the most northerly station of Peak Rail's development from Riverside station at Matlock (where there remains a connection to the national network).This view of where a new shed building is being erected was taken from Rowsley South station platform on 28 September 2005. *Les W. Perkins, courtesy of F. A. Wycherley/JCH*

BAKEWELL: This delightful rural scene shows the down-side station building, with the continuation of Station Road on the right.

On the beautiful spring morning of 10 May 2006 the station building can still be seen, but is now partly obscured by new construction. *Stan Roberts collection, copyright Peak Railways Association/JCH*

BAKEWELL station managed to reach its centenary, having been opened by the Midland Railway in 1862, but was closed to passengers by BR in 1967, and to goods the following year. In July 1966 a three-car Cravens Class 105 DMU from Derby leaves en route to Manchester Central, with the goods yard off to the right of the station.

Fortunately the building on the down side has mostly survived, part of which can be seen in the 'present' photograph taken on 10 May 2006; the bridge beyond links the two pictures. *Les Nixon/JCH*

HASSOP station also opened in 1862, being re-named 'Hassop for Chatsworth' at a later date, probably to meet the expectations of the Duke of Devonshire. It survived until closure to passengers by the LMS in 1942. This view of 4 June 1960, looking towards Bakewell, several years before the closure of the line, shows activity in the yard, controlled from the nearby signal box.

Today the station house remains on the right, while part of the down platform and the opposite part of the original buildings also survive, although subsequently added to, now occupied by the Country Bookshop and its excellent cafe, where the almond tarts can be particularly recommended! The 'present' photo was taken on 10 May 2006. *H. Townley, courtesy of J. M. Bentley/JCH*

MILLER'S DALE station opened in 1863, becoming 'Miller's Dale for Tideswell' from 1889 until 1965, when it reverted to the original title. Having celebrated its centenary, closure came shortly afterwards in March 1967. It was the junction station for Buxton (5½ miles away) – in 1947 on weekdays there were 16/17 trains in each direction, the journey only taking 9 minutes in the up direction and 10 in the down. The station was rebuilt in 1905 with five platforms, and in our picture of 19 April 1951 ex-Midland Johnson 2F 0-6-0 No 58224 heads east, with a 4F 0-6-0 in the background on a goods train, while a down train departs, passing Miller's Dale Station signal box on the extreme left.

On 14 April 2006, we see that that the up and island platforms remain in situ, together with part of the upside buildings. The 'Monsal Trail', funded by Derbyshire CC, is very popular with hikers, and the third photograph shows the front of the station building with a food trailer – their home-made cakes are also highly recommended! *H. C. Casserley/JCH*

MILLER'S DALE: Re-built 'Royal Scot' No 46103 *Royal Scots Fusilier* arrives with a Manchester to St Pancras express on 4 August 1959; the engine was allocated to 14B (Kentish Town).

    Since closure of the line in 1968 there has been a considerable growth of trees and shrubs, as seen in the 'present' photograph of 14 April 2006. *Ron Robinson/JCH*

CHEE TOR TUNNEL NO 1 is 401 yards in length, still intact but today kept locked. On Easter Monday, 2 April 1956, 2P 0-4-4T No 41905 has just left the tunnel en route for Miller's Dale with the 11.30am from Buxton.

Fifty years later, on Good Friday, 14 April 2006, we see the closed entrance to the tunnel, now surrounded by considerable tree growth. The 'Monsal Trail' takes a detour round it. *Michael Mensing/JCH*

BLACKWELL MILL ICI WORKS: This fine photo of 'Peak' Class 45 No D128 with a St Pancras-Manchester Central express rounding the curve from Miller's Dale by Blackwell Mill Works was taken in April 1966, just over two years before the end of services. Off to the right is the northern leg of the triangle junction leading to Buxton, with Peak Forest Junction signal box nearby.

The exact location is now difficult to access, but the 'present' view shows the approximate equivalent view, taken from the lay-by on the A6 between Buxton and Bakewell. The cottages down below were originally built for railway workers. The line curving round in the centre of the photograph is from Peak Forest and forms the northern chord of the junction referred to above. *Les Nixon/JCH*

Around Peak Forest

GREAT ROCKS JUNCTION: On 20 April 1968, not long before the end of steam on British Rail, this enthusiasts' special is hauled by two 'Black Five' 4-6-0s, Nos 45100 and 44949, as it approaches the signal box.

On 14 April 2006, 38 years later, there has been considerable growth of trees; the signal box remains, almost hidden by branches and with the pitched roof having been removed. The trackwork appears to be little changed. *Gavin Morrison/JCH*

GREAT ROCKS JUNCTION: On 20 July 1997 Nos 37133 and 37057 pass Tunstead Works with loaded limestone heading for Oakleigh near Northwich.

Less than ten years later, on 14 April 2006, we can see the considerable changes made to the Works. *Both JCH*

PEAK FOREST: Looking towards Chinley on 25 October 1982, Class 25 No 25134 is returning with 6H46, the empty ICI hoppers from Oakleigh to Tunstead.

On Good Friday, 14 April 2006, the 'present' photograph shows the changes to the works: some buildings having been demolished and new ones built. Class 08 shunter No 08588 is stabled on the right together with Class 60s Nos 60034 and 60083. The 08 is in a very smart all-over-black livery with a red stripe, and the connecting rods also in red. *Paul Shannon/JCH*

CHAPEL-EN-LE-FRITH: The freight line from Chinley South Junction to Great Rocks/Tunstead passes beneath the former LNWR Buxton line. On 31 March 1984 a Class 25 is at the head of empty limestone hoppers from Northwich to Tunstead.

Once more there has been much tree growth in the intervening years to 20 September 2005 when Class 66 No 66035 was photographed with a train of MBA wagons. *Both JCH*

Hope Valley and the Hayfield branch

NEW MILLS CENTRAL has a long history dating back to 1865, when it was simply New Mills, not changing its name until 1952 so passengers would not be confused with the other station in the town, New Mills Newtown. The 'past' picture was taken on 1 February 1989, with Class 108 Derby Lightweight unit CH268 (53924/54278) forming the 1350 service from Manchester Piccadilly. Note the small signal on the bracket being in the 'off' position; units from Manchester that terminated here moved on to the stub of the Hayfield branch (just east of the station) and waited there until it was time for them to return to Manchester.

On 21 September 2005 Class 142 No 142047 leaves the station with a Manchester Piccadilly to Sheffield service. It will be seen that the semaphore signals have been replaced by a colour light, but apart from this change there has also been an operational alteration: terminating services now arrive at the up platform, then reverse into a siding at the Manchester end of the station, when necessary, to await their next turn of duty. *Both JCH*

HAYFIELD was the terminus of a short branch of just under 3 miles; built by the Manchester, Sheffield & Lincolnshire Railway, it opened to passengers in 1868 and to goods two years later, the latter to serve the developing textiles industry. The line became joint between the MS&L and the Midland Railway in 1869 under the name of the Sheffield & Midland Railway Companies Committee, later the Midland & Great Central Joint. It remained open to goods until 1963 and passenger traffic until 1970. On 28 January 1967 a two-car Metropolitan-Cammell unit (later Class 101) has arrived and the tail lamp waits to be carried to the rear of the train for the return journey to Manchester.

Today nothing remains, although it is possible that the information office on the left was built from the stone of the station building. On 7 June 2005 the link between the two photos is the George Hotel in the background. Most of the trackbed was converted by Derbyshire CC into the 'Sett Valley Trail'. *Gavin Morrison/JCH*

NEW MILLS SOUTH JUNCTION is where the line from New Mills Central joins that from Stockport (via the Hazel Grove chord) and from Northenden Junction. On 15 July 1979 'Peak' No 45146 is seen with the 1955 Manchester Piccadilly to St Pancras service. These workings were diverted via the Hope Valley line following closure of the route via Miller's Dale.

The 'present' photo, taken 11 May 2005, shows Class 66 No 66181 with empty MEA wagons returning from Ashburys to Dowlow. Note the changes in the track layout, the down turnout now being beyond the signal box. *Both JCH*

CHINLEY: Taken from the roadbridge at the east end of the station, looking west, we see Class 25 No 25140 at the head of empty ICI PHV limestone hoppers returning to Tunstead from Oakleigh on 22 July 1976; for a long period it was usual for these trains to consist of 18 wagons. As can be seen, there was then quite a lot of abandoned railway land.

Nearly 30 years later, on 13 September 2005, Class 170 No 170397 forms a Liverpool-Norwich service operated by Central Trains, while in the station can be just seen a Class 158 DMU heading for Manchester Piccadilly. All the waste ground has been built on and the track reduced from four to two. *Les Nixon/JCH*

CHINLEY's first station opened in 1867, and was replaced by one on the existing site in 1902. On the Midland main line between Manchester Central and London St Pancras, it was the junction for the Hope Valley line and a busy station both for passenger trains and freight, particularly coal traffic – the volume of stone traffic is a relatively recent development. In our 'past' picture, showing the east end of the station in May 1960, 8F 2-8-0 No 48080 approaches with loaded coal, passing Chinley Station South Junction signal box, while on the right is 2-6-4T No 42109 with an up passenger service.

Forty-six years later, on 3 May 2006, the scene is hardly recognisable. Apart from the total rationalisation of railway infrastructure to simple up and down lines, there has been considerable property development, but the large building to the right of the bridge remains as the link between 'past' and 'present'. Class 60 No 60094 approaches the station with loaded hoppers from Tunstead. *Ron Robinson/JCH*

CHINLEY: Ivatt 2-6-0 No 46485 has arrived with the 0959 local from Sheffield on 29 October 1966 – note the water column at the end of the platform. These engines were first introduced by the LMS in 1946, this particular one having the longer tapered chimney.

On 20 September 2005 we see the rear of Class 142 unit No 142028 forming a Manchester Piccadilly to Sheffield service. Although there has been considerable growth in trees and bushes, the bungalow behind remains to create a link with the 'past' picture. *Les Nixon/JCH*

CHINLEY: On 29 May 1938, looking east into the Derbyshire hills, LMS 4P Compound 4-4-0 No 1088 pulls out of the station with an eight-coach train bound for Manchester Central.

Twenty-two years later, on 25 June 1960, 8F 2-8-0 No 48135 is at the head of a limestone train from Tunstead to Oakleigh near Northwich, known locally as the 'ICI hoppers'. The engine was allocated at the time to Northwich shed. The main difference is the addition of new lights and the semaphore signals at the west end of the platforms.

The third view takes us forward to 30 July 1983, and double-headed Class 37s Nos 37197 and 37283 with loaded 'Peakstone' PGA hoppers from Dove Holes Quarry (Peak Forest sidings). There has been total simplification of the track, and the signal box, lights and signals are all gone. The station looks almost desolate, and only the central island platform is in use.

Finally, on 28 June 2005 Class 60 No 60013 *Robert Boyle* heads west with loaded modern JGA hoppers. The footbridge has been severed and only crosses one track, the remaining station building has gone (there is now a basic shelter) and the railway land to the right has been cut back and a new housing estate built. *H. Townley, courtesy of J. M. Bentley/David Holmes/JCH (2)*

CHINLEY: West of the station, looking back towards New Mills, Class 31 No 31434 is employed on 1E29, the 0841 Manchester Piccadilly to Cleethorpes train, on 9 June 1984. This would be a Saturdays-only service, although at that period Class 31s were used regularly on Manchester to Sheffield trains.

Apart from the tree and bush growth the scene has changed very little as Class 60 No 60047 in EWS livery heads a train of empty hoppers, no doubt returning to Peak Forest, on 28 June 2005. *Both JCH*

EAST OF CHINLEY: Looking west, ex-LMS 0-6-0 No 44250 (allocated to Trafford Park shed) is seen crossing over to take the Peak Forest line on 4 March 1961 at the head of a long train of four-wheel trucks, with two brake-vans at the front and one in the rear.

On 3 May 2006 Class 158 First Trans-Pennine unit No 158765, allocated to Neville Hill depot at Leeds, speeds east towards Sheffield. There has been track rationalisation and the semaphore signals have gone, but the Crown & Mitre pub on the right is a nice link between the two pictures. *Gavin Morrison/JCH*

WEST OF EDALE: BR Standard 2-6-0 No 78023 heads the 12.50pm Sheffield Midland-Chinley service on 3 October 1959. In the background to the right can be seen Horsehill Tor.

The view is unchanged more than 45 years later, as two-car Class 158 No 158762 approaches, heading east with a Trans-Pennine service on 3 May 2006.** *Michael Mensing/JCH*

EDALE: On 5 July 1983 a four-car Swindon Class 123 Inter-city unit, originally built for the Western Region, heads towards Manchester forming the 1321 Hull-Manchester Piccadilly service. The station was pretty bare even in 1983, having become an unstaffed halt in 1969. Opened way back in 1894 by the Midland Railway, it has seen continuous service ever since.

Again the scene is virtually unchanged today as Freightliner Class 66 No 66512 is seen on 3 May 2006 running light engine to the west. *Paul Shannon/JCH*

EARLE'S SIDINGS: On 27 April 1983 Class 37 No 37265 is ready to re-start after having been recessed with five Class 76 'Tommies', including Nos 76054, 76010, 76013 and 76036, eastbound to Booths Yard at Rotherham for scrapping. On the down line Class 47 No 47572 powers the 0718 Parkstone Quay-Manchester train. The sidings were named after Earle's Cement, which owned the works at Hope, later acquired by Blue Circle; as a result of a merger it became Lafarge in the early part of this century. The sidings next to the main line were always owned by the railway but named after the cement works.

Twenty-three years later, on 3 May 2006, the scene remains virtually unchanged as Class 170/6 No 170630 (built by Adtranz at Derby) is en route to Liverpool Lime Street from Norwich. *Gavin Morrison/JCH*

HOPE station started life in 1894 as 'Hope for Castleton', then 'Hope for Castleton and Bradwell' before settling down as 'Hope' in 1965. In April of that year Class 5 4-6-0 No 44888 gets the 'Right away' from the guard with the 1730 Sheffield Midland to Manchester Central service.

It is sad to see that when the 'present' photo was taken on 3 May 2006 the station buildings have all gone and we are left with little more than a basic platform. *Les Nixon/JCH*

HOPE: In March 1966 8F 2-8-0 No 48190 trundles downhill through the station with a Tunstead-Margam lime train, passing a local Sheffield-Manchester service in the station.

The attractive lattice footbridge remains, as Class 142 No 142020 departs with the 1045 Manchester Piccadilly-Sheffield local service on the beautiful spring morning of 3 May 2006. *Les Nixon/JCH*

BAMFORD station was opened by the Midland Railway in 1894, in what must have been a very sparsely populated area, but it has remained open and has celebrated its centenary! On 29 March 1983 Class 37 No 37130 heads east with five Class 76 'Tommies' (Nos 76016/021/023/026/012) en route to Rotherham for scrapping.

Today the station buildings have gone and the station is unstaffed. On 28 June 2005 Class 66 No 66551, operated by Freightliner Heavyhaul, brings a train of loaded limestone in HHA and PGA hoppers (since replaced by HIAs) for either Cottam or West Burton power stations. The semaphore signal has been replaced by a colour light, controlled from Grindleford signal box. *Gavin Morrison/JCH*

Right The station building on the down side was built on two levels, with an entrance off the road bridge, as seen on 15 March 1973. *Michael Mensing*

BAMFORD: On 26 April 1984 Class 40 No 40118 is at the head of a down parcels train heading for Manchester Piccadilly, which was a daily service from St Pancras and virtually the last regular train to run between the two stations, although 20 years later there was a period during the West Coast Main Line upgrading when Midland Mainline ran HSTs from Piccadilly to the capital, which was a pleasant opportunity for London-bound travellers to enjoy the Hope Valley line.

On the rather hazy day of 28 June 2005, Central Trains Class 170/1 No 170105 is eastbound for Sheffield and beyond. The siding, signal box (now preserved at Darley Dale) and semaphore signal have all gone, while the colour light signal on the left is under the control of Earle's Sidings box. *Both JCH*

HATHERSAGE: This evocative photo of Ivatt Class 2 2-6-0 No 46485 approaching the station with the 0939 Sheffield Midland to Chinley local, passing a 9F 2-10-0 on a pick-up freight, was taken in January 1964. The station was opened in 1894 by the Midland Railway shortly after the absorption of the Dore & Chinley Railway.

The sidings and signal box have gone, together with the semaphore signal. Class 170 No 170116 heads towards Sheffield with a Liverpool-Norwich service on 3 May 2006, while on the left-hand side is a new development ('Hathersage Park') of modern architectural style; the units include a health club and various business premises. *Les Nixon/JCH*

GRINDLEFORD: On 5 July 1983, looking west, we see the interesting combination of Class 40 No 40141 and Class 25 No 25296 with 6E41, the 0354 Ditton to Sheffield Broughton Lane service conveying liquid oxygen for the steel industry, passing the signal box.

More than 20 years later, on 28 June 2005, Class 170 'Turbostar' No 170399, built by Adtranz/Bombardier, approaches the station with a Liverpool Lime Street to Nottingham service. *Paul Shannon/JCH*

GRINDLEFORD: This atmospheric photo shows 8F 2-8-0 No 48744 with a permanent way train as it shunts from the up main to the up sidings on a snowy day in February 1966.

Without trespassing into the remaining yard (with four sidings used from time to time by track maintenance machines), the exact view is not possible, so the 'present' picture, dated 3 May 2006, is taken from the end of the platform seen in the 'past' picture, looking east as Class 66/6 No 66603, operated by Freightliner Heavy Haul, coasts through the station. The sidings on the up side have all gone, as has the goods shed on the down. *Les Nixon/JCH*

GRINDLEFORD: By the roadbridge over the railway stands the old railway booking office, waiting room, etc, opened by Midland Railway in 1894. In the photo of around 1900 several horse-drawn conveyances await passengers.

As can be seen in the 'present' picture of 3 May 2006, the building remains exactly as it was, but is now a very popular café offering welcome refreshment to both railway travellers and hikers. The conversion took place after 1969 when the station was de-staffed. *Courtesy of Grindleford Cafe/JCH*

GRINDLEFORD station originally had platform buildings on both sides of the line. On 27 June 1963 we see ex-LNER 'B1' 4-6-0 No 61372 with the 12.45pm train from Sheffield Midland to Chinley.

On 8 July 2005 Class 158 DMU No 158760 is working a Trans-Pennine service from Cleethorpes to Manchester Airport; operated by Arriva Trains Northern, the unit is allocated to Neville Hill (Leeds) depot. Modern station lighting has been installed, but with the verdant surrounds the scene has changed very little. *David Holmes/JCH*

Buxton (LNWR) to Ashbourne and the Cromford & High Peak Railway

BUXTON (LNWR): Buxton was one of the few places where stations from rival companies were side by side. Undoubtedly unusual for two competing companies, the styles were virtually identical and perhaps one can put this down to the authorities in Buxton wishing to keep them in tune with the architecture of the spa town. Both were opened in 1863, one by the Midland Railway and the other by the Stockport, Disley & Whaley Bridge Railway, which was to become part of the LNWR in 1866. The undated 'past' photograph was taken from the end of the Ashbourne platform of the LNWR station, and to the left is the Midland station. A DMU can be seen in the latter, so we know that the picture was probably taken in the mid-1960s. The Ashbourne line closed to regular passenger services in 1954, but the platform continued to be used until at least 1964 for stabling, including the evening Buxton-Manchester Mayfield parcels.

The Midland station closed in 1967 and today there is not a trace. The curved Ashbourne line of the LNWR station has been removed (approximately where the two vans are parked), so the 'present' photograph was taken from the nearest possible position in February 2006. *Lens of Sutton/JCH*

HIGHER BUXTON station was opened by the LNWR in 1894, and, despite being very close to Buxton station (only half a mile away, and less by road) it survived until closure in 1951. In June 1930 '18 inch' tank engine No 6899 is seen on the 1.45pm train to Ashbourne. The engine carries shedplate '20', which was the code for Buxton Midland shed.

The line survives as a freight-only branch (just under 5 miles in length) to the industries at Hindlow/Dowlow – British Lime Industries Hindlow (aka Briggs) and Lafarge Dowlow. The 'present' photo was taken from the nearest bridge on 14 April 2006, as the 'past' picture was taken at platform level, which no longer exists. The links are the bridge beyond the train and the building beyond the bridge. *E. R. Morten/JCH*

LADMANLOW: Although passengers were conveyed in a type of brake-van on this LNWR-backed line from 1833 to 1877, there was no station or even a platform. Originally the line ran as far as Whaley Bridge, but was cut back in 1892, leaving Ladmanlow situated at the end of a short branch from Hindlow, on the Buxton to Ashbourne line. The sidings included two used by ICI. On 25 April 1953 beautifully turned-out ex-Midland 0-6-0 No 43618 is being admired by the passengers of the special train.

Although the railway sidings are long gone, the cottages remain, as seen in the 'present' photo of 14 April 2006.
R. M. Casserley/JCH

PARSLEY HAY was the junction where the line to Ashbourne left that to Friden and beyond (the Cromford & High Peak line). Opened in 1833 (although not really a station at that time), it went through a closure and re-opening after the line was re-aligned north of Parsley Hay in 1894, before it was replaced by the second station in 1899. In our 'past' picture, taken on 27 June 1964, ex-LNER 'B1' 4-6-0 No 61360 is at the head of a seven-coach RCTS special (with a Gresley buffet car in the centre) as it approaches Parsley Hay.

The line closed to regular passenger traffic in 1954 and eventually the trackbed has become a very popular walking and cycling trail. As seen in the photograph of 21 September 2005 there has been considerable tree growth, but the curve in the trail, beyond the larger trees, shows where the railway ran. *Gavin Morrison/JCH*

PARSLEY HAY: A brake-van special of 30 April 1967, with former Ministry of Supply 0-6-0STs Nos 68012 and 68006 at the head, stands at the station while enthusiasts are given the opportunity to take photographs.

Today the bridge remains but the tree growth is gradually changing the view of the embankment, as seen on **21 September 2005.** *Gavin Morrison/JCH*

ALSOP-EN-LE-DALE station was opened in 1899 and lasted until 1954, with excursion and occasional winter services to 1963. In the view of the station taken in 1952, looking towards Buxton, we can see that the buildings were of wood construction; note the semaphore signals, which tell us that there was a signal box nearby. It was a passing place, and the single track can be seen at the far end. At the time of the photo the station nameboards included Alstonfield (2½ miles away); as with all the intermediate stations, the local population was very small.

Apart from the roadbridge at the Buxton end of the station, the shape of the trees on the right is unmistakeable in the photograph taken well over 50 years later on 16 August 2005. *R. S. Carpenter (D. Ibbotson collection)/JCH*

Right Looking south towards Uttoxeter on 7 August 1953, ex-LMS Fowler-designed 2-6-4T No 42368 is at the head of the 10.10am train from Uttoxeter to Buxton. *H. C. Casserley*

ASHBOURNE: The first station was opened in 1852 by the North Staffordshire Railway, closing in 1899 to be replaced by a joint NSR and LNWR facility. As seen in the undated 'past' photo, the station was quite substantial with bays and station signal box. There were modest train services to Buxton to the north and Uttoxeter to the south, including through carriages on some trains to Manchester London Road/Mayfield. The line closed to regular services in 1954, with excursion and freight traffic until 1963.

Today the site of the station is a car park, but the Beresford Arms Hotel is an excellent link between 'past' and 'present', as seen on 16 August 2005. *Lens of Sutton/JCH*

FRIDEN: The Cromford & High Peak Railway was completed in 1831, leased by the LNWR in 1862 and absorbed by that company in 1887; complete closure came in 1967. Friden was the normal interchange location for services from Buxton and Middleton, and on 22 July 1966 one of the regular Middleton locos, 'J94' No 68006, is on the right, while to the left is Ivatt 2-6-0 No 46465 waiting to return to Buxton; the driver is looking back, no doubt wondering where the shunter has got to! The tenders are likely being used as mobile water tanks.

Today there is nothing of the railway to be seen (apart from the tops of rails sticking up in the foreground) but we can see the chimney of the brickworks beyond the car park. *Les Nixon/JCH*

MIDDLETON TOP: This wonderful photograph was taken on 30 April 1967 (the last year of operation) from an area that is no longer accessible, and shows the whole complex and two of the 0-6-0STs (ex-Ministry of Supply 'J94s') used on the line, Nos 68006 and 68012.

Today the area is a popular tourist attraction, as seen in the lower-level 'present' picture taken on 16 August 2005, showing the car park and visitors' centre with the chimney and main engine house building in the background. The inset shows a nearby surviving railway sign. *Les Nixon/JCH (2)*

Buxton (LNWR) towards Manchester

BUXTON: This historic photograph is taken from a postcard (posted in 1916) and shows how close together the two stations were – the LNWR to the left and the MR to the right. The occasion was undoubtedly early in the First World War when a battalion of soldiers, perhaps from the Sherwood Foresters (Notts & Derby Regiment) appear to be arriving – note the two officers on horseback. The soldiers on the left look remarkably young. The LNWR sign details places to where tickets can be bought, including Stockport, Manchester, Liverpool, Oldham, Halifax, Bradford, Sheffield and Glasgow.

Today's photo shows the side of the former LNWR station on 10 May 2006, but it is hard to believe that the Midland station was so close. The area to the right of the LNWR building is now a car park and a new road, completely obliterating where the Midland station stood. *Glynn Waite collection/JCH*

BUXTON: On 22 March 1987 the diesel depot by the side of the station contains Class 47 No 47152, and two Class 37s are also visible. Locomotives were used primarily for stone trains from the nearby quarries, and stabled between turns of duty, with up to a dozen engines present over a weekend.

The depot was subsequently closed and the locomotives now use the stabling point at Peak Forest. On 7 June 2005 we see the disused building as Class 156 No 156421 leaves for Manchester. *Both JCH*

BUXTON station was opened originally by the Stockport, Disley & Whaley Bridge Railway in 1863, subsequently passing to the LNWR, the LMS and eventually BR. On 7 August 1953 Fowler 2-6-4T No 42315 awaits departure with the 1.10pm train to Manchester London Road. To the left is the Ashbourne platform. At the end of the line in the centre can be seen the well-known 'fan window'. *R. M. Casserley*

BUXTON: The same scene on 4 September 1980 has Class 128 Gloucester parcels car No M55990 on the left and various Class 104 BRCW units.

Comparison with the 'present' photograph shows that the canopy on Platform 2 has been cut back and demolished completely on Platform 1. The Ashbourne platform too has gone. On the left is Class 156 No 156425 and to the right 'sister' unit No 156421 in the modern livery. Services are all to Manchester Piccadilly, with some extended to Blackpool or an occasional one to Southport. *Brian Morrison/JCH*

BUXTON: To the right of the diesel depot were sidings used by DMUs or locomotives, as seen on 1 March 1983, with three Class 104 units stabled. The short Starting signal dominates the picture.

Today's comparison, taken on 7 June 2005, shows the deteriorating building on the left and the sidings empty and becoming overgrown, but with the same signal and signal box now visible in the distance. *Gavin Morrison/JCH*

BUXTON STEAM SHED had the code 9D, under Longsight (9A) in Manchester. On 4 March 1961 we see a variety of locos, including two passenger tank engines, two 8F 2-8-0s, two post-Grouping developments of Midland 0-6-0s, Nos 44327 and 44461, and two ex-LNWR 0-8-0 goods engines. The shed was a six-road dead-end building, opened in 1892, enlarged in 1935 on the closure of the Midland shed, and finally closed in March 1968. The author visited the shed on 10 May 1953 when there were no fewer than 52 engines present, of 11 separate classes, the oldest being Nos 58083/4, two 1P 0-4-4Ts of Johnson Midland design introduced in 1881.

After closure the building was completely demolished and nothing remains. However, the land has not been re-developed, as seen on 7 June 2005. *Gavin Morrison/JCH*

CHAPEL-EN-LE-FRITH station, on the line from Buxton to Manchester, dates back to 1863. In the 'past' picture, looking towards Buxton from a Manchester-bound train on 7 August 1953, the station is well-kept, with the signal box at the end of the platform.

On 20 September 2005 Class 150 No 150142 arrives with a Blackpool service. The signal box has been replaced by one on the other side of the line, but the station building remains much the same and is now in use as a restaurant. *R. M. Casserley/JCH*

Below The road side of the station building is seen in LNWR days. *Lens of Sutton*

WHALEY BRIDGE station has remained open since 1857, serving a small town famous for the Peak Forest Canal, where buildings survive from 1832. The undated 'past' photo was taken when the platform-mounted signal box was still open.

The scene is not so different on 20 September 2005; the station is still well-kept as Class 150 No 150142 departs with a Manchester to Buxton service. *Lens of Sutton/JCH*

FURNESS VALE station also opened in 1857, and two members of the station staff pose for this undated photograph, looking towards Manchester. There is little tree growth so we see a number of buildings clearly.

Photographed in the rain on 26 August 2005, Class 150 No 150145 leaves forming the 0817 service from Buxton to Manchester Piccadilly. The large building on the left remains, although now mostly obscured by trees. *John Williams collection/JCH*

Great Central to Dinting, Glossop, Hadfield and Woodhead

DINTING is the junction where the branch to Glossop leaves what used to be the GCR main line over Woodhead to Sheffield, and has a history dating back to its opening in the 1840s. On 17 September 1980 Class 76 No 76001 approaches the station with a special Warrington-Tinsley freight. These engines became the mainstay of the line following electrification in 1954.

Twenty-five years later, on 1 July 2005, while there is still double track over Dinting Vale viaduct, the former main line to Sheffield is now singled as far as the end of the branch at Hadfield. Class 323 EMU No 323236 is about to take the line to Glossop on the left. *Paul Shannon/JCH*

DINTING: A 'Hadfield' unit, with car No M59404M leading, calls en route from Glossop to Manchester on 1 May 1981. These Class 506 EMUs were introduced in 1954, and were stabled and serviced at Reddish depot.

Although the lines to Glossop and Hadfield have been singled, the station buildings and platforms remain, and today the line is operated by Class 323 EMUs, three-car sets built by Hunslet, the first of which entered service in 1992. On 1 July 2005 No 323229 is bound for Glossop. While the remains of the down platform and building can just be seen, they are almost hidden by the growth of trees and bushes. *Both JCH*

DINTING: In this third picture of what was formerly the main line over Woodhead, two Class 76 'Tommies', Nos 76007 and 76012, rattle past Dinting Station signal box with a train of westbound loaded coal hoppers on 1 May 1981. The track was double at that time from Hadfield.

By 1 July 2005 it is single line and the up side platform has almost disappeared. In the distance can be seen a Class 323 on the east side of the triangle, heading for Hadfield from Glossop. The signal box has been refurbished with modern windows. *Both JCH*

GLOSSOP: On 23 August 1984 'Hadfield' unit No M59608M can be seen at the platform awaiting departure for Manchester Piccadilly. The station began life in 1845 simply as Glossop, having 'Central' added in 1922, but reverting to the original name in 1974.

Apart from the change of name, the entrance to the station remains much as before, with some alteration to the right-hand entry with removal of the stones at the top and a door added, as seen on 7 August 2005. The normal pattern of working is for trains to arrive from Manchester and reverse out to Hadfield, then return to Glossop before leaving for Manchester, although there are some services that call first at Hadfield before going on to Glossop. *Noel Machell/JCH*

HADFIELD: The 'past' view of the station is looking towards Manchester and shows a very well-kept location. The station opened in 1844 and was known as 'Hadfield for Hollingworth' in some timetables, which is what is shown on the station nameboards in this photograph. A signal box can be seen on the right-hand side beyond the footbridge, with a semaphore signal in the distance.

Coming forward to 1 July 2005, Class 323 No 323236 is arriving, before returning to Glossop, then on to Manchester. Apart from the singling of the track, the up-side platform and buildings remain much the same, although the station has been refurbished. The down-side platform and buildings have disappeared. *Lens of Sutton/JCH*

HADFIELD: Looking east from the end of the up platform, Class 76 Nos 76009 and 76023 are approaching the station with a short rake of MCV and MCO mineral wagons on 17 September 1980.

On 1 July 2005 the scene is unmistakeable, with the same gantry and the hillside on the right – sadly, however, it is now the end of the line. *Paul Shannon/JCH*

WOODHEAD: This wonderful panoramic view, looking west, shows how the railway was built along the Longdendale valley. On 18 June 1981 a pair of Class 76s are employed with a mixed goods train heading towards Penistone. The tank wagons at the front of the train are European-registered, probably on their way to the Harwich-Zeebrugge train ferry. The station can be clearly seen and, in the distance to the right of the pylon, is Woodhead Reservoir, the first of a chain towards the west. *Paul Shannon*

WOODHEAD: On 22 August 1980 Class 76 No 76051 is setting back with an empty coal train; the up line through the tunnel is closed, so it will proceed eastwards 'wrong line'. The modern-looking signal box can be seen by the parked cars. The station was opened in 1844 and closed in 1964. As can be seen, the platforms were staggered, having been rebuilt in 1954, the year that the electrification was completed. As there is virtually no population in this exposed spot one wonders whether the station was intended primarily as a staff halt .The last regular passenger service ceased in 1970 and the line closed completely in July 1981.

On 7 August 2005 we see that the house remains but the other buildings have all been demolished, although part of the up-side platform is still there. It is clear where the trackbed once ran. *Both JCH*

INDEX OF LOCATIONS